P9-DTL-513

BILLIE JEAN KING

Photo Credits: Bruce Curtis
Published by Creative Educational Society, Inc.,
123 South Broad Street, Mankato, Minnesota 56001
Copyright © 1976 by Creative Educational Society, Inc. International
copyrights reserved in all countries.
No part of this book may be reproduced in any form without written
permission from the publisher. Printed in the United States.
Distributed by Childrens Press,
1224 West Van Buren Street, Chicago, Illinois 60607

Library of Congress Number: 75-38966   ISBN: 0-87191-479-4

Library of Congress Cataloging in Publication Data
Morse, A. R.   Tennis champion, Billie Jean King.
SUMMARY: A biography of the tennis champion who has been
a leader in making an equal place for women in athletics.
1. King, Billie Jean—Juvenile literature.   2. Tennis—Juvenile literature.
(1. King, Billie Jean.   2. Tennis—Biography)   I. Title.
GV994.K56M67   796.34'2'0924   (B) (92)   75-38966
ISBN 0-87191-479-4

TENNIS CHAMPION

BILLIE JEAN KING

by a.r. morse

CREATIVE EDUCATION MANKATO, MINNESOTA

4

Billie Jean King is a woman with a lot of fire
in her. Some call it passion. Others call it strength.
Billie Jean herself says, "I always felt I could be
great." By the time Billie Jean was 5 years old, she
had a strong feeling inside her. She didn't know
what she would be. But she was sure about one
thing. She would leave her mark wherever she
went.

6

A mark she has made. Billie Jean King has become the greatest female tennis player in the world. She attacks a tennis ball with power and force. She's a scrambler and a fighter on the court. She has won more championships than anyone else. And she has helped many other women in their sports' careers.

1890596

"Jillie Bean," as Billie Jean is sometimes called, plays without fear of being hit by the ball. Being fearless, she has learned to rush to the net. There, she can smash the ball before it bounces. With steady practice, her volley has become a fast flash in the air.

"The way I play — it's me," Billie Jean says with a laugh. Her bright eyes dance behind her large round glasses when she laughs.

Billie Jean seems tough to some people. Yet often she's very shy. She stares at her feet when people clap for her. She doesn't like parties. And often Billie Jean feels unsure around strangers.

At the same time, Billie Jean is a ham. If she gets a microphone in her hand, she loves to tell jokes. And she can't resist sticking out her tongue before photographers.

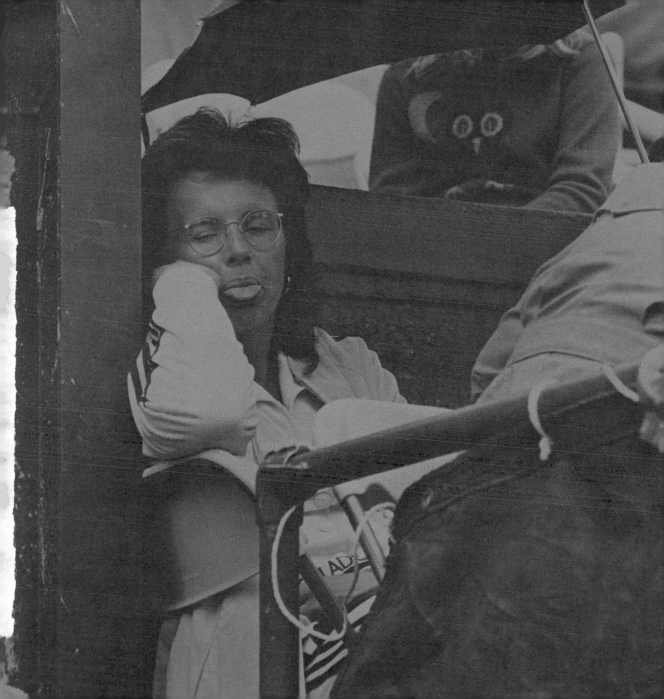

Billie Jean grew up liking many different sports. She was born a natural athlete. When she was only 2, Billie Jean learned to play catch with her father. At 11, Billie Jean decided to quit football and baseball. She thought the boys wouldn't like her. She could hit harder and run faster than many boys.

Then Billie Jean's father suggested she try tennis. She tried it. And she loved it. Immediately, Billie Jean set out to become the greatest tennis player in the world.

Not everyone likes Billie Jean. People sometimes boo when she wins a match. They think she wins too much. They cheer for the younger players, such as Evonne Goolagong or Chris Evert. Billie Jean remembers that people cheered for her when she was young. "It would be nice," Billie Jean said, "to get an odd cheer or two now. But the people seem to think that I don't care."

18

Smack! In the pocket of her racket. That's where Billie Jean likes to hit the ball. It feels right. It looks right. And the tingling feeling deep inside her tells her it *is* right.

Billie Jean makes a fresh start in every game. There's always the challenge to make the ball do what she wants. And there's always the chance for the perfect shot. That's why tennis is such an exciting, alive sport for Billie Jean.

Tennis is like life, Billie Jean says. Sometimes you win. Sometimes you lose. There are ups and downs. Good days and bad days.

Billie Jean often wonders about what she's doing. What good does it do to play a sport for a career? Does it do anything for anybody? Even when she wins, Billie Jean asks herself these questions.

Tennis *is* important, Billie Jean decides. She sees that when she plays tennis well, she inspires people. She makes others want to go out and play well, too.

"Winning is fun," she says. "But the real joy comes from the fun of playing." When fans watch Billie Jean serve, they want to reach for the sun on their serves, too.

Billie Jean thinks fans should make a lot of noise when they're watching a tennis match. Usually there is a hush over the courts. People often wear only white clothes. Billie Jean would like to see these things disappear. She says those things make tennis "too proper."

Billie Jean would like to see more noise and more color. It's no wonder that there's always a colorful, noisy crowd following Billie Jean.

There was really a lot of noise at one match. Billie Jean had challenged Bobby Riggs to a tennis match. The prize was $100,000. Winner take all.

Millions watched the match on TV. Thousands watched it in the stands at the Houston Astrodome. Everyone wanted to see who would win.

Male tennis players usually hit the ball harder and faster than women. For that reason, many thought that Bobby Riggs would beat Billie Jean. But Bobby was almost twice as old as Billie Jean.

On the night of the match, Billie Jean played as if she were on fire. The "King" overcame Riggs and won the match.

Happy that the big match was over, Billie Jean hugged her husband Larry. Larry King is Billie Jean's manager and handles much of their business. Larry feels proud of his famous wife. Sometimes he even calls himself "Mr. Billie Jean King."

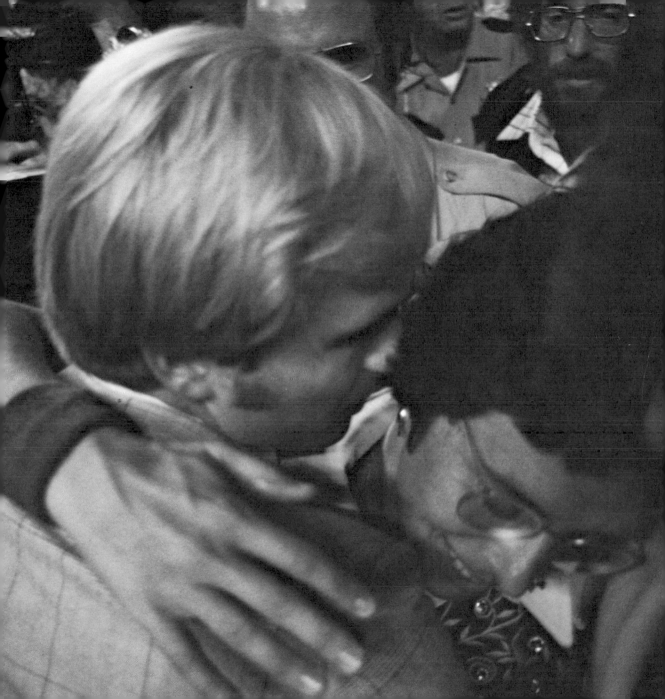

30

Billie Jean King is happy with her image. She's made people take women seriously in tennis. She's shown them that women can be athletic and still be women. And Billie Jean has proven a point. She has shown that it's most important to be and do what you want. Not what others think you should be. Billie Jean King has made her mark.

BILLIE JEAN KING
EVEL KNIEVEL
O.J. SIMPSON
HANK AARON
THE ALLSTARS